Table of Contents

I0170513

Experimental Recipes for the New Year

Simple Experimental Meals to Try in 2021

BY: Ida Smith

License Notes

This book is licensed for your personal enjoyment only. This book may not be re-sold or given away to other people. If you would like to share this book with another person, please purchase an additional copy for each recipient. If you're reading this book and did not purchase it, or it was not purchased for your use only, then please return to your favorite ebook retailer and purchase your own copy. Thank you for respecting the hard work of this author.

Introduction

With 2020 rolling out, it is alright to make a grand entry with simple experimental recipes for your family. If you think you have tried many recipes and would love to try your hands on new stuff, then you are welcome to read on. All you need is to grab a cup of coffee, rest your back and discover experimental dishes to try in 2021.

Recipe 1: Experimental ham and cheese waffle

Make no mistake about it, you should make several twists in your waffle recipes, and this is just another tasty style to try.

Ingredient List:

- 6 toaster waffles, frozen
- ½ pound ham
- 3 tbsp. butter, unsalted and melted
- ¼ pound cheddar cheese, lightly sliced

Preparation:
Arrange the toaster waffles on a platter
Place the ham, cheese, and the other waffles over it

Drizzle the melted butter over it

Return the waffles to the skillet you used in melting the butter, sauté them for 5 minutes till the cheese melts

Transfer to plates and serve warm

Have fun!

Preparation Time: 10 minutes

Cooking Time: 5 minutes

Total Time: 15 minutes Yields: 4 servings

Recipe 2: Cheesy cake twist for a new year

Looking for an easy but soft sweet cheesecake? Make this recipe one of your go-to cheesecake with just 6 ingredients.

Ingredient List:

- 6oz cream cheese, finely softened
- 6oz whipping cream, sweetened
- 12oz condensed milk, sweetened
- ½ cup lemon juice, fresh
- 2 strawberries, halved
- 2 lemon wedges
- A piece graham cracker crust

Preparation:

In a clean large mixing bowl, stir in the whipping cream, cheese, milk, and mix with a hand mixer

Add the lemon juice and continue mixing till well blended

Pour content over the cracker crust and sit in the refrigerator for 1 hour

Garnish with lemon wedges and berries

Have a blast!

Preparation Time: 10 minutes

Freezing time: 1 hour

Total Time: 1 hour 10 minutes Yields: 5 servings

Recipe 3: Experimental chocolate cake for 2021

Who would ever say no to chocolate cakes, especially when they come so soft and melty! 2021 shouldn't be welcomed with the usual chocolate recipes when you can try this easy twist.

Ingredient List:

- 1 cup all-purpose flour
- ½ tsp. baking soda
- ¼ cup cocoa powder
- A pinch of salt
- 1 cup. sugar
- sunflower oil
- vanilla extract
- white vinegar

Preparation:

Preheat oven to 300 degrees

Combine the flour, baking powder, cocoa, sugar, and salt into a baking pan

Add the vinegar and oil, stir well to mix

Pour in some water and work it to blend with a fork

Bake in the ready oven for 35 minutes or till it bakes through, with the toothpick coming out dry

Allow cooling in a wired rack

Serve later with joy!

Preparation Time: 8 minutes

Cooking Time: 35 minutes

Total Time: 43 minutes Yields: 6 servings

Recipe 4: Banana experimental ice-cream

Bananas are sweet, no doubt about that but they are even sweeter when combined with cocoa. And they have sweet promises for the year with plans to excite your taste buds. So, feel free to try your hands on this.

Ingredient List:

- 2 bananas, peeled and frozen
- cocoa powder
- peanut butter
- vanilla extract

Preparation:
Toss all ingredients into the food processor, pulse it till it turns creamy
Pour into jars and add whatever toppings you desire. From strawberries to cookies, fresh fruits, etc.
Serve with love!
Preparation Time: 5 minutes
Additional time: 5 minutes

Total Time: 10 minutes Makes 2 tall jars of ice cream

Recipe 5: Spicy potato boats

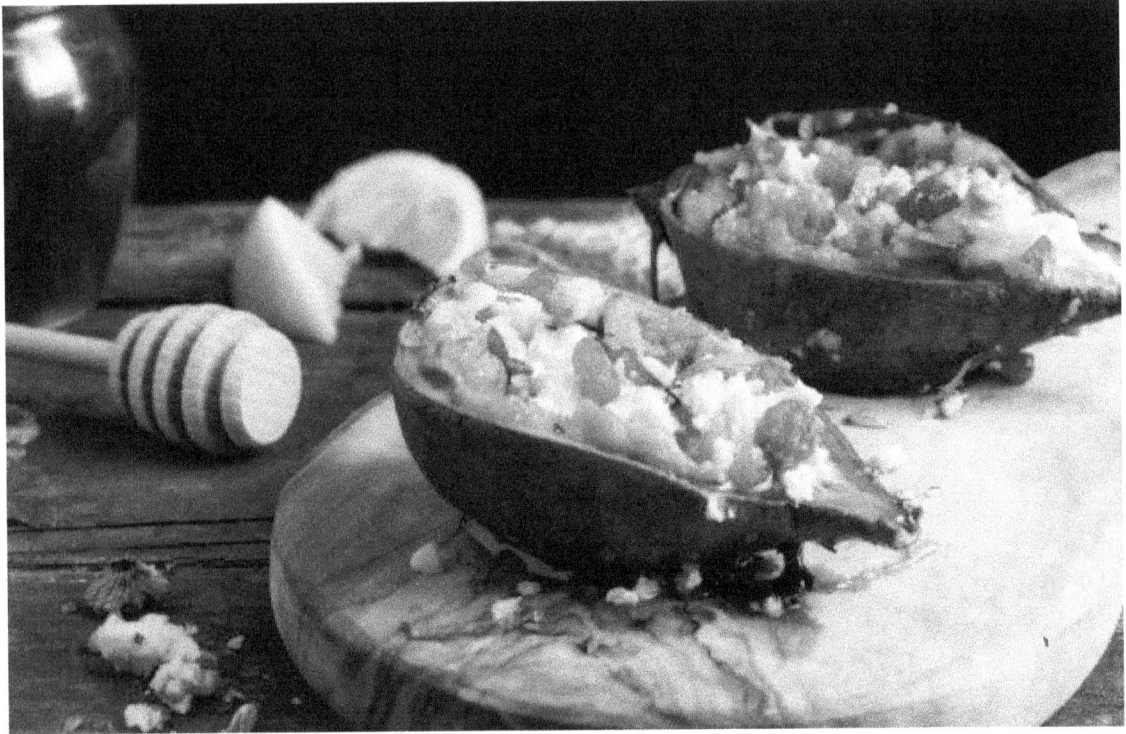

This dish will leave you and your family coming back for more.

Ingredient List:

- 2 sweet potatoes
- ½ cup black beans, drained
- 1 small avocado, peeled and mashed
- ½ tsp. ground cumin
- ½ cup corn, frozen
- ¼ tsp. cayenne pepper
- ½ cup salsa
- ½ tsp. sea salt
- fresh ground black pepper

Preparation:

Make holes with a fork on the sweet potato and microwave them for 9 minutes

Cut potatoes in halves, remove the inner portions, set aside

In a small bowl, mash the avocado, inner portion of the potato, and cumin, and cayenne pepper

Stuff each potato boat with the mashed content followed with salsa, corn, and beans. Drizzle the salt and pepper over it

Serve with love!

Preparation Time: 10 minutes

Cooking Time: 9 minutes

Total Time: 19 minutes Yields: 4 potato boats

Recipe 6: Spicy Watermelon tart

Spicy and tasty meals are a great way to start the year, and watermelon comes all prepared to welcome 2021 sweetly.

Ingredient List:

- 7 strips of watermelon rind, frozen
- 1 onion bulb, diced
- 2 jalapenos, nicely diced
- 2 sweet peppers, sliced
- 2 tbsp. coconut oil
- 8-ounce coconut milk
- A pinch of salt
- Jamaican curry
- sweet corn

Preparation:

Over moderate heat, pour oil into a clean nonstick skillet

Toss in the watermelon rinds and sauté for 10 minutes

Stir in the cut onion, peppers, salt, and jalapenos. Sauté for 5 more minutes or till translucent

Add the coconut milk, cook for 2 minutes and drizzle the curry over in. stir to mix and simmer for 3 minutes

Add the sweet corn, cook for 1 minute and turn off the heat

Scoop into plates and serve

Have fun!

Preparation Time: 10 minutes

Cooking Time: 12 minutes

Total Time: 22 minutes Yields: 4 servings

Recipe 7: Crispy eggy chorizo tacos

Crispy taco bites will always be loved for their crunchiness and if you love to try new recipes, give this a chance. You will fall in love with every bite.

Ingredient List:

- 3 large eggs
- 4 corn tortillas
- ½ pound fresh chorizo
- feta cheese, crumbled

Preparation:
Over medium heat, stir chorizo into a nonstick skillet and cook through. Drain and set aside
Crack and toss the eggs into the skillet, scramble it to your desire or poach it
Warm your tortillas in the microwave or toast them lightly in a saucepan

Lay tortillas on a platter, top it with the eggs, cheese, and any veggies you like Enjoy!

Preparation Time: 10 minutes

Cooking Time: 15 minutes

Total Time: 25 minutes Yields: 4 servings

Recipe 8: Chicken tasty rice soup

Chicken is perfect for every meal and if you are looking for new experimental ideas for rice, then try this soup in the new year.

Ingredient List:

- sunflower oil
- white flour
- 1 cup chicken, diced
- ¼ cup carrots, chopped
- 1 tbsp. chopped celery
- 1 package, long grain wild rice
- 6 cups Chicken broth
- ½ cup chopped red onion
- 1 cup heavy cream

- ½ tsp. black pepper
- salt
- 1 tsp. curry

Preparation:

Over moderate heat in a nonstick saucepan, pour the oil and stir in the onion, celery, carrots, and curry. Sauté for 6 minutes

Pour in the rice, flour, and chicken broth, cook for 17 minutes

Heat the heavy cream in another saucepan and add to the cooking content

Add the cooked chicken and cook for 35 minutes or till the rice cooks through.

Serve warm with delight!

Preparation Time: 10 minutes

Cooking Time: 57 minutes

Total Time: 1 hour 7 minutes Yields: 8 servings

Recipe 9: Experimental potato pancake

How do you like your pancakes? With bananas, ripe plantain, or oats. Well, here is a plate of healthy sweetness promised you from sweet potatoes.

Ingredient List:

- 1 cup mashed potato
- 1 large egg, beaten
- ½ cup parmesan cheese
- olive oil
- 2tbsp fresh chives, chopped
- A dash of cinnamon
- ½ cup white flour

Preparation:

In a clean large bowl, combine all the ingredients. (except chives) Add some water to get your desired consistency

Over medium heat, drizzle the oil into a large nonstick skillet and pour in a scoop of the batter.

Flip over from time till golden brown

Lay them on a plate, garnish with chives and sour cream

Have fun!

Preparation Time: 10 minutes

Cooking Time: 25 minutes

Total Time: 35 minutes Yields: 5 servings

Recipe 10: Crunchy baked chicken

Here is a perfect toast for 2021 and if you are starting the year with a party, then welcome your guests with this toast of crunchiness.

Ingredient List:

- 4 chicken laps
- 3 large eggs, beaten
- 2 cups bread crumbs, toasted
- 1 cup pecans
- black pepper
- coconut oil

Preparation:
Preheat oven to 300 degrees

Prepare the baking tray with baking paper and spray

In a clean bowl, combine the pecans, pepper, with bread crumbs, set aside

Wash the chicken, pat dry, and paint with the coconut oil.

Dip the chicken in the egg and roll it over the crumbs. Place on the ready baking tray

Bake in the oven for 1 hour till it turns brown and crunchy

Allow cooling before serving

Have fun!

Preparation Time: 10 minutes

Cooking Time: 60 minutes

Total Time: 1 hour 10 minutes Yields: 4 servings

Recipe 11: Eggy experimental pork chops for 2021

You may have tried several pork chop recipes but this cheesy twist is every tasty and a good way to eat pork in the coming year.

Ingredient List:

- 1 cup panko
- 2 large eggs, beaten
- 5 (4oz) pork chops
- garlic salt
- cayenne pepper

Preparation:

Preheat oven to 350 degrees

Season the pork properly with salt and pepper

Dip each in the egg bowl, and toss it over the breadcrumbs

Lay in the baking rack and coat with the cooking spray

Bake in the oven for 30 minutes

Allow cooling for 4 minutes

Serve with desired vegetable or dipping sauce

Have fun!

Preparation Time: 15 minutes

Cooking Time: 30 minutes

Total Time: 45 minutes Yields: 5 servings

Recipe 12: Sesame breadsticks

Have you ever doubted what cheese and sesame seeds could do on bread? Try your hands on this promising tastiness and light up your bread taste for 2021.

Ingredient List:

- 2 cups Self-rising flour
- instant yeast
- 30g melted and cooled unsalted butter
- ¼ cup sunflower oil
- 195ml warm water
- salt
- sesame seeds

Preparation:

Preheat oven to 300 degrees

Toss all ingredients into a dough mixer, work it for 5 minutes at low speed. When it is well mixed, cover the bowl with wet cloth and leave it to sit for 60 minutes. Alternatively, mix all ingredients in a big bowl, add the water gradually to you achieve a firm dough.

Knead the dough till it becomes stretchy and firm, cover with wet cloth and sit it for 1 hour.

On a floured surface, roll out the dough, flatten it and cut into thin strips. About 25cm long and 1cm wide

Lay the cut strips on a prepared baking tray, paint them with oil, sprinkle sesame seeds, and bake for 25 minutes

Remove from the heat and sit for cooling

Serve with love!

Preparation Time: 15 minutes

Cooking Time: 25 minutes

Additional time: 1 hour

Total Time: 1 hour 40 minutes Yields: 20 breadsticks

Recipe 13: Spinach-cheesy chicken roll-up

Did you know the versatility promised in chicken would end up as a roll-up meal? Here is another chicken wrap of deliciousness to pamper your taste buds.

Ingredient List:

- A handful of baby spinach
- 3 slices of boneless chicken breast
- sea salt
- ¼ cup feta cheese, crumbled
- black pepper
- fresh oregano, chopped
- Cooking spray

Preparation:

Preheat oven to 350 degrees

Spread the chicken breasts on a baking tray

Lay the spinach, oregano, and cheese over it

Roll each chicken into a bundle and secure with a toothpick

Drizzle the pepper, salt, and cooking spray over it. Stand it for 2 minutes before slotting it into the oven

Bake for 25 minutes, transfer to the rack for cooling

Serve with a glass of wine

Have fun!

Preparation Time: 20 minutes

Cooking Time: 25 minutes

Total Time: 45 minutes Yields: 5 servings

Recipe 14: Turmeric potato scones

How do you like your potatoes? You probably haven't had plans for turmeric in the coming year, right? Well, here is a combo you don't want to miss. Let's try it.

Ingredient List:

- 700g gram potatoes, washed and chopped to cubes with the skin
- 1 tsp. turmeric powder
- 40g cream coconut, grated
- kosher salt
- ground black pepper

Preparation:
Boil and drain the cubed potatoes
Add the grated cream coconut, turmeric, salt, and pepper to the potatoes

Mash them till well blended. Scoop into patties and lay on the baking tray or grilling grate

Bake or grill for 8 minutes

Eat warm or cold

Have a blast!

Preparation Time: 8 minutes

Cooking Time: 28 minutes

Total Time: 36 minutes Yields: 10 servings

Recipe 15: Avo-pistachio ice cream

In 2021, you can try out an avocado-themed ice cream even if you are not a kid. Especially when you had a hectic day.

Ingredient List:

- 1 large avocado
- 600ml pistachio milk
- ½ cup dates
- 100g pistachios, unshelled
- honey syrup

Preparation:
Toss all ingredients into a blender and puree it to a smooth pulp
Add the honey or maple syrup

Empty into a jar and stand it in the freezer for 1 hour or till it freezes

Remove from the fridge and serve when ready

Enjoy!

Preparation Time: 10 minutes

Freezing time: 1 hour

Total Time: 1 hour 10 minutes Yields: 4 servings

Recipe 16: Vodka coconut milk pasta

If you are receiving 2021 with optimism, then a great way to spice your appetite is trying something new and extraordinary.

Ingredient List:

- 1-pound pasta (any), cooked and drained with water preserved
- ½ vodka
- 18-ounce can tomato sauce
- 4 garlic cloves, nicely minced
- ½ cup extra virgin olive oil
- 14-ounce can coconut milk
- salt
- black pepper
- red pepper flakes

Preparation:

Over medium heat, pour in the oil, add the garlic and fry till tender

Toss in the tomato puree and the vodka. While stirring, add the coconut milk and sauté for 5 minutes

Fold in the pasta with some of the drained water and cook for additional 3 minutes

Scoop into plates and serve warm

Have fun!

Preparation Time: 10 minutes

Cooking Time: 15 minutes

Total Time: 25 minutes Yields: 6 servings

Recipe 17: Cheesy baked ziti

Pasta seems to promise all the delight in the pantry world and with 2021 insight, it will be wonderful to try new pasta recipes. So, if you are a lover of new stuff, here is another thrill awaiting your taste buds.

Ingredient List:

- 1 pack ziti noodles, cooked and drain according to instructions
- 20 ounces jar spaghetti sauce
- 1-pound ground beef
- 2 cups Mozzarella cheese
- garlic powder
- A pinch of salt

Preparation:
Preheat oven to 300 degrees

Toss the beef into a skillet and cook till it browns

Stir in the garlic powder, salt, and keep turning till the beef browns and cooks through. Drain it and add the spaghetti sauce and noodles

Empty content into a baking dish and spread the cheese over it

Place a foil over it and bake for 35 minutes or till cheese melts

Dish into plates and serve warm

Have fun!

Preparation Time: 20 minutes

Cooking Time: 55 minutes

Total Time: 1 hour 15 minutes Yields: 7 servings

Recipe 18: Experimental cookies

Do you love cookies? Then, you can try this simple and easy cookie recipe, it is something you've never seen or tasted.

Ingredient List:

- 2 cups almond flour
- vanilla extract
- ½ tsp. baking powder
- ½ cup maple syrup or honey

Preparation:

Preheat oven to 200 degrees

Whisk the almond flour and baking powder into a clean bowl, add the maple/honey syrup and vanilla

Work a small, sturdy dough and cut into round cup-like patties

Arrange them on a baking tray and bake for 14 minutes

Leave for cooling and serve

Have fun!

Preparation Time: 15 minutes

Cooking Time: 14 minutes

Total Time: 29 minutes Yields: 10 servings

Recipe 19: Experimental ant on the long

Ants aren't so annoying when they give a pleasant meal inspiration. If you have kids, they will love this and you can ditch peanut and use hummus for a lingering delight.

Ingredient List:

- 6 celery stalks or carrot stalks
- ½ cup peanut or hummus
- ½ cup raisins or dried fruits variety

Preparation:
Wash and cut celery into halves, if using carrots, cut them into halves too
Spread the hummus or peanut butter over them
Place the dried fruits, pecans, nuts, and whatever fruit you like
Have fun!

Preparation Time: 10 minutes
Total Time: 12 minutes Yields: 4 servings

Recipe 20: Biscuit sweet gravy

Biscuits are super tasty but when they are combined with other vegetables, you can wish for a swell 2021.

Ingredient List:

- butter
- 8 baked vegan biscuit or any biscuit you like
- ½ cup. White flour
- 3cups milk
- 14oz sausage, crumbled
- ¼ tsp. garlic powder
- 1 tsp. oregano
- salt
- cayenne pepper
- ½ cup. Parsley, chopped

Preparation:

Melt the butter in a medium saucepan, toss in the sausage and sauté for 6 minutes

Stir in the flour and milk, whisking till it boils and thickens

Add the salt, pepper, garlic, and other ingredients. Cook till it thickens

Lay the biscuit on a platter and pour the gravy over it

Top with the chopped parsley

Serve with joy!

Preparation Time: 12 minutes

Cooking Time: 10 minutes

Total Time: 22 minutes Yields: 5 servings

Recipe 21: Experimental fruit pizza

Pizza seems to be everyone's favorite and in the coming year, you can make a fruity burst of sweetness with it. Cheers to a pizza of flavors!

Ingredient List:

- 1 batch cookie dough
- 3ounce mandarin segments
- 4 fresh kiwis, sliced
- ½ cup cream cheese frosting
- 3ounces grapes, halved
- 2ounces blueberries
- 2ounces raspberries, halved
- 6ounces strawberries, hulled and halved

- honey

Preparation:
Preheat oven to 300 degrees
Place dough in a pizza pan and bake for 15 minutes or till the edges gets a little tanned
Leave crust to cool while you prepare the fruits if you didn't
Spread the cheesy frost over the crust and start the fruit layering
Glaze it with soft honey
Enjoy!
Prep time 19 minutes
Cooking Time: 15 minutes
Total Time: 34 minutes Yields: 3 servings

Recipe 22: Nutty energy bars for 2021

Energy bars are incredible energy providers and if you are looking for new recipes to start your busy schedule with, try this.

Incredible

- 1 cup dates, pitted
- ½ cup maple syrup
- ½ cup almond butter
- 1 ½ cups rolled oats, toasted
- 1 cup roasted nuts, almonds, pecans, etc.
- ½ cup. dried fruits

Preparation:
Stir dates into your food processor and work it to form a small dough

Combine the oats, nuts, dates, and dried fruits in a bowl

Heat the butter and maple in a saucepan and add to the dried content

Mix all ingredients and pour over a paper-lined tray

Spread it over the tray, cover with a cloth, and set in the refrigerator for 30 minutes or more

Remove from the refrigerator and cut into bars

Serve happily!

Preparation Time: 10 minutes

Cooking Time: 10 minutes

Additional time: 30 minutes

Total Time: 50 minutes Yields: 12 servings

Recipe 23: Beefy experimental new year casserole

Let the sparks of joy be seen on the faces of your loved ones as you serve them this tasty beefy meal on new year's eve.

Ingredient List:

- 1 (14oz) package beef
- 1 (12oz) can black beans, drained
- ½ cup tomatoes, crushed
- 1 (12oz) can corn, drained
- 1 pack. Taco seasoning
- 1 cup. vegan cheese
- 1 cup. salsa
- 2 cups frozen tater tots

Preparation:

Preheat oven to 360 degrees

Cook beef in a nonstick skillet till it turns brown

Stir in the seasoning, beans, tomatoes, and corn. Sauté for 3 minutes

Add the salt, pepper and sauté for 2 minutes

Pour content into a baking tray

Top it with the frozen tots, making a pattern if you wish

Bake for 30 minutes, remove from the oven and drizzle the cheese over it

Return to the heat and bake for 5 minutes

When the cheese is melted, remove from the oven, allow cooling

Cut into plates and serve

Have fun!

Preparation Time: 15 minutes

Cooking Time: 40 minutes

Total Time: 55 minutes Yields: 10 servings

Recipe 24: Tasty fried rice, vegan-style

Even if you are not vegan, you can give some healthy fried rice a try. And if you are looking for a different taste in fried rice, then here is a recipe to try.

Ingredient List:

- 1 cup. Rice. Cooked according to package instructions
- garlic powder
- ½ cup corn kernel(can)
- sunflower oil
- 1 red onion bulb, nicely diced
- ½ cup peas(can)
- 1 carrot, diced
- soy sauce

Preparation:

Pour the oil into a large skillet, when hot, toss in the diced onions, carrots, garlic powder.

Stir in the peas and corn, sauté for 3 minutes

Add the cooked rice, soy sauce and simmer for 5 minutes

Dish into plates and serve

Have fun!

Preparation Time: 13 minutes

Cooking Time: 10 minutes

Total Time: 23 minutes Yields: 4 servings

Recipe 25: Peasy-creamy experimental potato salad

Do you think you are fond of potatoes? Well, here is a super tasty and creamy twist of a salad that will make potatoes win a medal in a race.

Ingredient List:

- 2 potatoes, boiled, skinned, and cut into cubes
- ½ cup celery, nicely chopped
- 1 can chickpeas, drained and rinsed
- 1 red onion bulb, diced
- ½ cup dill, fresh and chopped
- ½ cup mayo
- fresh lemon juice
- ½ tsp sea salt
- black pepper
- whole grain mustard

Preparation:

In a small bowl, mix the mayo with mustard, pepper, salt, and lemon juice. Set aside

In a large glass bowl, combine the potato cubes, mayo mix, and veggies. Stir well and pour into plates

Serve with delight!

Preparation Time: 12 minutes

Additional time: 5 minutes

Total Time: 17 minutes Yields: 4 servings

Recipe 26: Mexican-styled quinoa for 2021

Have you recently fallen with quinoa? Here is a grand way to thrill your taste buds in the coming year and have quinoa to love always.

Ingredient List:

- 1 cup frozen corn kernels
- 3 cups cooked quinoa
- 1 ½ tbsp. cumin
- 1 can. organic beans
- 1 cup jarred salsa

Preparation:

Pour corn and black beans into a large skillet, sauté for 4 minutes or till content tenders

Stir in the quinoa and cumin, cook for 4 minutes till quinoa gets crunchy

Fold in the salsa and continue stirring till well combine and content looks dry

Remove from the heat, leave for cooling
Serve with love!
Preparation Time: 15 minutes
Cooking Time: 12 minutes
Total Time: 17 minutes Yields: 4 servings

Recipe 27: Experimental tofu mix of tastiness

Do you love tofu? You can try out something new and tasty with just 3 ingredients and be happy with your creation.

Ingredient List:

- 1 block tofu, diced
- 4 handfuls of baby spinach
- 1 cup bruschetta

Preparation:

Over moderate heat in a medium saucepan, stir in the bruschetta, add the tofu and sauté for 6 minutes or till liquid evaporates

Fold in the spinach, simmer for 4 minutes or till it shrinks

Remove from the heat and serve it warm

Have fun!

Preparation Time: 10 minutes
Cooking Time: 12 minutes
Total Time: 22 minutes Yields: 3 servings

Recipe 28: High-protein lentil soup for 2021

Get ready to stuff your health with all the protein it needs to stay fit and fine in the coming year. And if you crave lentils, here is a recipe to experiment with.

Ingredient List:

- 1 large red onion, nicely diced
- 2 carrots, diced
- rosemary
- 1 cup lentils
- A handful of celery, roughly chopped

Preparation:
Over moderate heat, pour1/3 cup of water into a saucepan
Add the onions and carrots and cook till it caramelizes and the water evaporates

Stir in the rosemary and lentils. Cover and cook for 25 minutes or till the soup thickens

Viola! Soup is ready

Serve warm or cold

Have fun!

Preparation Time: 15 minutes

Cooking Time: 30 minutes

Total Time: 45 minutes Yields: 3 servings

Recipe 29: Tasty experimental pea soup

Pea soups are the delight of vegans and everyone who loves good health. And if you are looking for a sweet touch on peas as the year rolls out, here is a recipe to try.

Ingredient List:

- 1 medium onion, finely chopped
- 500ml, vegetable broth
- coconut oil
- 3 garlic cloves, nicely minced
- A handful of mint leaves
- frozen peas
- salt
- black pepper
- 1 cup cashew milk

Preparation:
Over moderate heat, pour the oil, little water and sauté for 2 minutes
Fold in the onions, cook till tender. Add the garlic and sauté for 1 minute
Stir in the peas, broth and cook till peas defrost
Pour content into a blender and blend till smoothen
Return to pan, add milk, salt, pepper, and simmer for 1 minute
Turn off the heat, dish into soup bowls, and serve warm
Have fun!
Preparation Time: 15 minutes
Cooking Time: 6 minutes
Total Time: 21 minutes Yields: 5 servings

Recipe 30: Kiddies and pea nuggets

Do you have kids, or you are hoping to host a pool party in 2021? Here is one of the tastier bites that your guest should have, and it is super simple to make.

Ingredient List:

- 1 cup rolled oats
- 1 cup panko, toasted
- ½ tsp. garlic powder
- 1 (12 ounces) can garbanzo beans. Undrained
- salt
- onion powder

Preparation:
Preheat oven to 350 degrees

Stir in the oats into the food processor and blend it into powder. Turn the flour into a bowl, set aside

Drain the chickpeas (keep the liquid) and pour into the food processor with the salt, onion, and garlic. Pulse it for 3 minutes and set aside

Add ¼ cup of the drain chickpea liquid into a small cup, whisk it till it turns foamy, and add to the oat flour

Fold oat mixture into the food processor and pulse till it forms a ball. Add more chickpea liquid to get the desired dough-like consistency

Cut content into nugget shapes, roll over the panko, and lay on the prepared baking tray

Bake for 15 minutes

Leave out on the rake to cool and serve with any dipping sauce

Have fun!

Preparation Time: 20 minutes
Cooking Time: 20 minutes
Total Time: 40 minutes Yields: 7 servings

Conclusion

Trying new dishes comes with lots of enthusiasm and anxiety but with these simple and easy recipes, you can try new dishes and be proud of your creation. Similarly, as you are ready to receive 2021, it will be to treat yourself and your loved ones to tasty and healthy dishes. So, feel free to experiment on all and enjoy a fruitful year. Cheers!

Don't miss out!

Visit the website below and you can sign up to receive emails whenever Ida Smith publishes a new book. There's no charge and no obligation.

https://books2read.com/r/B-A-LRXL-EZBLB

BOOKS 2 READ

Connecting independent readers to independent writers.

Did you love *Experimental Recipes for the New Year: Simple Experimental Meals to Try in 2021*? Then you should read *Baby Boomers - Recipes with Memories: Baby Boomer Recipes that Build Today's Culinary World*[1] by Ida Smith!

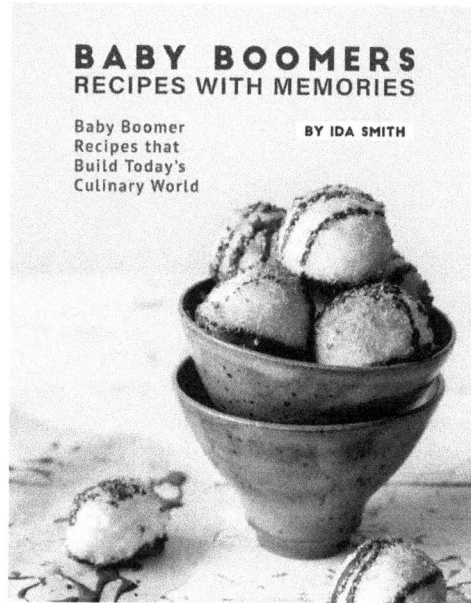

Remember the day when mum would actually make dinner. You did not buy, it was made from scratch, and it was super healthy and delicious. In the days of cookbooks that transcend from generation to generation, flavors were built upon and enhance the past. Baby Boomers have a life that many will not understand, and the foods that still look mouthwatering weird.

1. https://books2read.com/u/b5k78k

2. https://books2read.com/u/b5k78k

www.ingramcontent.com/pod-product-compliance
Lightning Source LLC
Chambersburg PA
CBHW081300040426

42452CB00014B/2591